T0067889

FROM
DARKNESS
TO
LIGHT

The Anxiety & Depression of a Troubled Poet

KING DRE PENCASSO

authorHOUSE®

AuthorHouse™
1663 Liberty Drive
Bloomington, IN 47403
www.authorhouse.com
Phone: 833-262-8899

Published by AuthorHouse 10/20/2022

ISBN: 978-1-6655-7421-1 (sc)
ISBN: 978-1-6655-7420-4 (e)

CONTENTS

PREFACE

Ever since I was a kid, I've wanted to write my own book of poetry to tell the story of my life and everything I experienced before the age of eighteen. I often write about life, love, happiness, and other things that people can relate to— being taunted every day because of my physical appearance, unexplained drama with my family, or the things that have fueled my anxiety and depression. For years, people have told me that I have a gift that's more powerful than I could ever imagined. and I thought it was about time to actually listen to them.

I've been perfecting my passion for poetry since I was nine years old, but only during high school did my passion get stronger, due to the abusive household that I was living in at the time. My whole point in writing this book is to tell my story in hopes that it'll touch a life in the best way possible, as if it were a song. I know mental health has been a topic of discussion during the past few years, so I thought it would be helpful to share my story with who that can relate to my struggles with depression, anger, and anxiety. I've battled with all three as a kid, and it only became more intense and obvious throughout my teen years. I still have my struggles today, but I've learned how to cope with them through art, meditation, and other things that help keep me from wanting to take my life or lash out in anger.

All I am is a poet with a story looking to help those battling the same war as I am, in hopes of keep them from going down the same path or experiencing the same struggles I did. To anyone this book may impact, I thank you for allowing me to be of any assistance to you, and I hope it helps you through your battles as well. You're never alone, although at times it may seem that you are. With that being said, I hope you as the reader not only indulge in my story but also take away motivation from it. I strongly thank you in advance for taking the time to read my first official book.

I was inspired by my mother, Trena Kennedy, to write poetry and also by the talents of Tupac Shakur (2Pac), Maya Angelou, Earl Simmons (DMX), Langston Hughes, Pablo Picasso (hence my name being Pencasso), and Lawrence Parker (KRS-One). I can be followed on Instagram @ kingpencasso803, Facebook @Dre Pencasso, and Snapchat @drepencasso803.

TAUNTED FOR AMUSEMENT

Life was a nightmare from the beginning. No father figure
    to show me the ropes,
just the nature around me or a close cousin who meant the
    most to me.
I moved around nonstop, trying to move out of the nest,
with a mother devoted to having the best but already full of
    stress,
and neglected by a father who never truly cared for me,
saying "I do" only to be divorced years later because of
    infidelity.
I would say it started in school, but that would be a lie,
ignoring that my own kin were already giving me a reason
    to cry—
especially an aunt who never cared for me without a legit
    purpose
but showed me what it's like to see clowns at the circus.

Let's fast forward to school, where I'm surrounded by other
   kids

and I'm the topic for jokes. But it is what it is.

I'm a skinny kid with crooked teeth and beetle-like eyes.

I just want to know why they insist on analyzing

me because I'm different from them. But who knew

an ugly kid like me would have so much hell to grow through?

I mean, I know some people taunt you for their own
   amusement.

While developing a temper that I came close to losing,

I questioned God often: Why? Why me? What did I do to
   deserve this hate?

How much pain and hell does a young man like me have to
   take

before they break down and call it quits, putting an end to
   it all?

Crawling in my own blood, I saw my demon's shadow on
   the wall.

Voices in my head told me to come to the dark side,

cause the real world is toxic, and I'd have peace on the dark
   side.

That was just the beginning. Things got worse in middle
    school,
right before word got out about my mom,
all because a kid told the school she was gay for kissing a
    female,
like it was his business to even tell.
Just chose to talk about me because he was getting roasted
at the back of the bus. Then his laughter changed
to seriousness, and he put my business in the spotlight.
I tried being the quiet kid, but that only lasted for so long
before the hell around me just wouldn't leave me alone,
adding more fuel to the fire inside of me.
It further fed the demon that was breeding inside me.

I walked into the house to face my biggest devil of all
in the form of a guardian taking his rage out on me.
Even my bad grades shouldn't result in abuse to me,
bruises and sore bones from the broomsticks I was struck
    with.
Now I bring that pain with me through life. I'm stuck with it.
I'm an angel in disguise, with the rage of a demon.

LETTER TO MY ADDICTION

Under your control, I've destroyed myself and the places I've
    called home,
made childish mistakes that forced me to be alone,
went from being a loving kid to a grumpy adult, and
numbed feelings from within but caused damage as a result.
All my life, I've been looking for the wrong medicine
to cure this feeling or even to erase my past's skeleton.

Then one day, I came across a pill to neutralize the hurt,
so I pushed happiness away, only to make the pain worse.
At the time, I was dealing with my sister going missing
and an ache in my mouth that I was too stubborn to fix.
In most cases, you'd take a pill or two for temporary relief,
but I was consuming ten and wouldn't stop until this "cure"
    was complete.

In the meantime, I was acting out toward those I cared the
   most for,

getting help through efforts only an uncontrolled slave would
   ignore.

They don't know what I'm battling, but I refuse to speak,

showing signs of desperation in how addictive ways would
   tweak.

Caught myself in the mirror a few times, but I don't recognize

the figure looking back at me with the hell in his eyes.

Then you said to me, "Why would I let you go when I'm
   winning the war?

I turned you against your own kind, even gave you a scar.

My mission is to not only destroy you but everything that
   you cherish,

and I've completed my goal when I see you perish!"

Hard to admit, but I blame myself for letting you have it
   your way.

I saw the sun in the distance, but I turned away

to head down a path that consisted of rain and sorrow.

Demons look appealing, and of course I'm tempted to follow,

thinking maybe it's for the best when I reach the end.

Only fools party in the dark. The process of forming friends

with the worst intentions in the world caused self-destruction.

You were looking for happiness but ran into an interruption.

And in the midst of it all, you taught me more about myself

and why I was looking at myself through the eyes of everyone
    else
who saw me as someone that appeared lower than them—
hence your confidence in the beginning was way overcome.
So I thank you for teaching me that self-love was the key
to reaching a better me—to set myself free.

I've changed for the better, with mistakes along the way,
but they made me the great man that I appreciate today.
We parted ways for good, if God is willing.
Will I look in the dark in hopes of forming another friend?

FAILED SUICIDE

It was the summer of 2016. I remember the event so vividly:
at war with my former self as well as my past insecurities,
allowing the jokes from my childhood to fuel my self-hate,
making me more hesitant to look at my own face.
I've heard it all before: crooked teeth with the big eyes,
boney like an addict, or even E. T. in disguise.

Let's continue the story from the previous chapter. Let's dive
    deeper.
The attempt to take my own life was when I was weaker.
Around 2 a.m., I was in the bathroom, full of tears,
hand full of pills, and tired of unanswered prayers.
In my mind, I could've ended it all, then I would've been
    good.
But I was tired of living a lie, being happy but misunderstood.
I was in a depressed mess. All I needed was help to escape.
I would've left right away, if heaven were a mile away.

I sat up and grabbed my bottle of aspirin,
with ten pills left to consume, before collapsing.
Then I drifted off to this light. It showed signs
that I'm here for a reason, and right now isn't my time.
I listened to the message with my eyes rolled in the back of
    my head,
no pulse to be found. I appeared to be dead
before I came back to the surface. I gasped for air,
got up on my feet. All of a sudden, I'm well aware
of my existence and the impact of my presence,
bringing happiness to my loved ones. To them, I'm a blessing.

Then a voice in my head said, "You're a gift, my child!
Look at my blessings for you, then you shall smile.
Everything that you've been through will soon be understood,
and once you start to smile, you will truly be healed!"

"You're right," I said. "I apologize for hating your creation.
I saw life as a failure without the consideration
of the higher power that blessed me with this life,
but I placed life in the wrong hands for the wrong people to
    decide
how I choose to appreciate the one gift that we're blessed to
experience, in hopes of it being beautiful."

When the sun comes up and the stars go to sleep,

that lost soul will soon rise to its feet
to push a little further, no matter the challenges ahead
or the doubts that continue to dwell in his mind—
the one who looks for new ways to shine
through the darkness and bless the world with light
as he awakes every day to continue the fight.
He refuses to give up or let the bad vibes prevent
his search for happiness and this thing we call life.

TORN FAMILY

I was naive to the truth way before I even knew that I was
    hated by the people

who share the same genes as me though we are far from the
    same.

You may ask, "Where does this hatred stem from?" or perhaps,
    "What created these vibes?"

In my mind, it's just a matter of people feeling entitled to
    certain things

or feeling as though they're better than you in ways
    unexplained.

When you follow along with me, you'll begin to understand
    my pain. Ever since I was a kid,

I've felt out of place with these people that call themselves
    "family."

It's sad to see how churchgoing "Christians" have driven this
    heated vibe out of me.

I wouldn't wish this madness on my own worst enemy, or fuel
those I disagree with with such bad energy.

And I won't mention a dad who never took the time to
properly raise his son in a cold world, leaving his side
before he even turned a year old.

You made a vow under God to love and honor your wife,

but I see it meant nothing to you—can't provide a life for your
seed that could've turned out to be beautiful.

And to add insult to injury, I find out I'm not your only child,

and I'm not even behind the reason you smile. Yeah, it's foul
when I think about it,

because it made me blame myself for my dad not wanting me,
as if I caused all this pain.

As a result of his absence, I'm left with the urge to forge a
bond with someone else,

who may not understand why I come around so much because
I didn't have anyone else.

I'm in a house full of adults, with one of them making my
presence seem like such a disgrace,

then you make my mom feel unwanted, which to me is a slap
in the face. So what? She was gay,

and so is your only son, but you embrace him with love—
that's when the carnage was begun.

Greatest family in the world, at least for a time. That's what
I was fooled to believe before life as I know it was shown

to me after the truth came to light. I'm already going through
    hell at school, and the last

place I need it is at the same place I lay my head. Throughout
    the drama, I get close

to a cousin who's just like me but more distant, before I was
    old enough to see the obvious on display

right in front of me. We developed a bond, although I was
    most hated by the same person who

gave him life when she told my mother that I'd never amount
    to anything in my already sad life,

but I'm lost trying to understand what I did to deserve such
    negativity. I was consistently accused

of doing things that I never actually did, like taking movies
    of my liking when I was actually

granted permission. Because of her, to this day, I refuse to go
    home to rekindle a brotherhood

that's been separated since high school, but it's no love lost—
    we all grow apart sometimes.

In fact, we reconnected through Facebook, reassuring me that
    our motto still exists: "Us against the World."

Let's be honest about one thing: my family died in the nineties,
    along with my great-grandparents.

There's been no love found since then, and it taught me that
    we're not family,

although by blood we're kin. My family is my enemy, but this
    rivalry wasn't started by me. I'm

just the only one willing to stand on that energy. I'm not able
    to fake how I felt for all these years,
after hearing so many things that made me look at them in a
    totally different light. If I had it
my way, I'd trade it all just to bring back Mom and Dad for
    at least one day, if it means it'll spark
the peace to forever take the pain away.

CONTEMPLATED MURDER

Last night I had a dream: I did something that you wouldn't
    believe.
But close your eyes and drift off as I paint out this scene:
I'm not a killer by any means, just possessed with crazy ways.
That man put his hands on my mama. That made me go
    insane.
I walked in my room, grabbed my gun, and loaded it up;
walked into her room with the goal to send him up,
visions of brains all over the wall with blood all on the floor.
Did him a favor; now he can't breathe no more.
Call the paramedics and the cops. Yes, I am guilty
cause a man felt that you could play with my only family.
Man of the house I will always and forever be,
even if he feels like he can get one up on me—
backed me into a corner, so it's kill or be killed.
I'm paranoid, but I try to keep the peace overall,
just in case I'm tested to make the rain fall,

cause he doesn't value life in its capacity as he should.
I made my presence known, but it still may be misunderstood;
establish my stance so he can never get it confused,
or he'll be the next breaking headline on the news
with the source of death being the result of stupidity,
just another fool thinking he can ever replace me.
Fell down and hit your head, better yet you tripping;
he thought he was bad, but now he sees his clothes leaking.
But the crazy part of it all, I never wanted to do it.
Just get mad at yourself for being cocky and foolish.
Thought everything was sweet because I choose to remain
    quiet,
but you jumped on the wrong one, which led to a riot.
Far from a street guy, you thought you could easily defeat me,
but I know way too much. The pain in life was training me
in the backyard with my brother educating me,
turning me into a master of emotions.
I'm dangerous. I can punch a wall but won't feel a thing,
knuckles scratched up with the rage flowing in my veins.
Tried to turn me against my mom—it's a part of your scheme
just so you can force me out then create a crime scene,
manipulate her, then take everything away from her,
cause you know her love would give you anything.
Talks in the living room, saying how she needed a break
and that I should get out more—I'm too comfortable in my
    place.

Comparing my life to yours when you got kicked out into
    the streets
for trying to be grown, then you got what you wanted.
But I'm nothing like you; I'm too grounded for the streets.
Must be thinking I'm stupid, like I don't see what's going on.
You tried your best, and that's why I wanted to send you
    home.

FELL APART

I never thought that I would get to this point in life:
everything in question, even the things I really want in life,
crying to myself almost every night while battling anxiety,
asking, "Why me?" or better yet "Why does this pain keep
    attacking me?
Why must I continue to juggle alcohol mixed with painkillers?"
Blasting music in my headphones to distract my mind from
    the thriller
in the night, calling my name whenever I'm on the edge,
    prepared to jump
to my last breath, in hopes that I won't come back afterwards
    to explain
the motive behind my breakdown or even the failed suicide,
    cause I went insane.
So I keep my mouth closed to keep loved ones from the worry,
knowing well enough my well-being will always be the peak
    of their worry.

But who really cares that I'm an emotional mess barely holding on

by a thread? So I smile when they see me like on the inside I'm strong.

But I'm wrong for trying to take your King when he feels like he doesn't belong

on this planet cause he can't handle the hell on earth he's force to move in,

telling you to pray for me, cause deep down, Lord knows, I'm losing it.

I confess, I've been selfish every time I thought about cutting my lifeline off,

cause in my mind, I'm nothing, and losing me wouldn't even feel like a loss,

just another lost soul looking for death as the only exit to find peace,

based on a perception by pastors and the godly messages they taught me.

I was afraid of how you would look at me if I said I wanted to kill myself.

At the time, I thought the world was better off without me.

I'm sorry for almost taking myself away from you without you knowing why.

I'm sorry for wearing a fake smile just to avoid trying my best to cry.

I'm sorry for keeping you in the dark to keep you away from
the truth.

I'm sorry for turning to the influence of drugs hoping it'll
improve

my sadness, when in fact it's only used as another tired excuse

to avoid accountability when I needed help to overcome the
demon within

visiting me in the night that comes in the form of a close
friend.

Been at war with myself, and it's a roller coaster of emotions

from sadness to happiness, from smiles to tears.

But the evil forces never prosper, thanks to your prayers.

The journey isn't over, but it does get easier from this point.

Restart with a fresh mind, hoping that I don't disappoint

you again like I've done in the past with my antics,

flipping from hot to cold due to my uncontrolled mental
gymnastics.

The weapons formed against me were made by me

and handled by the pain of the past that took a toll on me.

Never again will the dark take control of me,

make me act out, or force my loved ones to give up on me.

I fought back from the attachment endured by the wrong
influences

with temporary happiness that will force the weak-minded
to lose it.

SELF-LOVE

I never *loved* myself:
    I've always hated how crooked my teeth were,
    my physique being so skinny without muscles,
    running from the ugliness of my smile,
    or even the distortion of my speech.

I never had *confidence*;
    I often spot the beauty of women in public,
    but never do I approach them for conversation
    because of the fear of rejection or being unable to respond,
    which causes me to admire from afar.

I envy my *brothers*,
    the attention they get whenever we hang out,
    whether it's from their appearance or their swagger.
    I'm there in existence but disappear when the spotlight
    shines upon them with the given eye candy.

The *absence of a father* means
 I wish I had the love of my dad in my life,
 and all my life I've searched for the reasons why
 he never bothered to be around,
 although his presence was never hindered
 even through his own infidelities.

The *impact of bullying* on me is
 I heard all the names in the book from peers,
 and my family treating me like an outcast.
 I became the sheltered, shying away from the crowd,
 hiding in the corner with a hoodie covering my face,
 zoned in music best describing my current mood
 when I was trying to fit in with those around me,
 mixed up in the street life, partaking in certain activities
 resulting in either a jail cell or the grave.

The *impact of an adult's decision* was
 one kiss in the club led to rumors being spread
 about the love life of someone far beyond school,
 but to avoid being embarrassed, from being roasted
 by jokes that hit the heart (and I won't lie, it inspired
 the hatred for my mother's lifestyle, being gay),
 I ignored that she was seeking happiness or even
 figuring out life, as we all do when we're placed
 in the real world to find balance along the way

LIFE REGRETS

Self-Belief

    I've always known the star that resided within me,
    but I never pursued the potential that others could see
    knowing my passion for words or the stories I told
    from the past experiences I've faced along the road.
    Words have impact, especially when it comes to mental
    health, helping to save those who seem lost like myself,
    looking for an outlet or something similar that they can
    place their emotions and feelings into

Self-Love

    I recall over a million times that I've faced myself
    in the mirror, only to be disgusted with the man
    looking back at me, not realizing that the man in
    the mirror is only a reflection of the scars that I
    have yet to heal or the damage consumed by fear
    that I have yet to remove with acceptance. I resemble
    the beauty of my mother, but I have several defects

that cloud my vision from seeing the King that indeed rests within me. Failed attempts to change who I was from dealing with females who made me think I wasn't a great man, all because I didn't fit the image of what they believe a "Good Man" looks like.

I Love You

Too many times have I buried the memories of friends I've lost over the years, but it eats me alive, knowing that I failed to express my love or care for them, being that they helped me in some of my worst times in life. Although many times I've shown my love through my actions, words sometimes could've been better to express how much I loved or appreciated them. more than they could ever realize I did.

I Apologize

I apologize to my heart for putting it through so much trauma that it didn't deserve, chasing after lessons in the form of a "love interest" that made me resent what my heart was truly built for.

I am who I am,
and who I'm not, I'll never be.

HOPE MY HEART FORGIVES ME

Forgive me for the pain and any errors I've created,
for I know you're pure and full of love, yet I've
underestimated your Greatness,
willing to put others first who've only used you as a replacement.
You stayed true no matter what I put you through
and truthfully, I don't deserve you.

What is love? I'm trying to define it with your greatness as a
    blindness
to those who desire real love, but at the circus they'll never
    find it.
So they see men like me as a target for amusement,
then make us feel like we're winning when in reality we're
    losing
a battle that we never thought we were in, being distracted
by smiles and fake gestures from a love interest to leave us
    stranded,

looking for answers as to what we did wrong cause we gave
    our all,

only to be left out in the cold, leading to unwanted cold
    hearts.

I was born with your blessing, but along the way we were
    separated,

with me still possessing your power without understanding
    the purpose

of something great beyond explanation, but several admis-
    sions caused a disturbance,

taking the attention away from the quality that it was built on.

So forgive me for all the wrong I've done to you. I'm a student

trying to love right, but in the process of being stupid

I've allowed many to misuse and even abuse you.

But at the end of the day, I still forever choose you

for all your flaws to the small beautiful things you do,

for allowing me to share. To make others feel beautiful

in the midst of a cold dark world, you still find ways to glow,

disregarding the scratches or bumps throughout the journey

of understanding the quality of your making.

BEFORE I PERISH

Before it's time to leave and my spirit moves on to a better
    place,
    let me smell those flowers while they're still blooming
    or even embrace the small memories that we make together,
    for they'll only be memories as a part of me, forever a part
    of our history.

Indulge in my hugs when you're lost within my love,
    laugh with me, dance with me, smile with me, live life
    with me.
    Until the end of time, with you in mind I can rest
    peacefully
    to smile eternally. I hugged you as if I never wanted to
    let go or talked to you as if I never wanted the conversations
    to end.

When the clock's out and we're no longer able to speak,
    I hope the times stay around so you can always
    look back with something to smile about,
    thinking of me every time a song or movie plays
    and then suddenly thinking of me and however I
    reacted through smiles or even crying.

Before I perish,
    don't let me go until you tell me you love me
    or let the memories dwell before you miss me.
    I shall not fade away before you embrace me.
    I shall not leave before reaching the love that awaits me.
    I shall not fly before I fully learn to crawl,
    then fully learn to walk without falling from grace.
    I shall not move on before correcting my wrongs:
    to live life freely instead of living through songs,
    to speak for my emotions that I don't give a voice to.
    In conclusion, just don't let me fly away to my home
    in the sky before you tell me how much I mean to you,
    and most important, don't let me fly away alone.

ACKNOWLEDGMENTS

As I celebrate this milestone in my life, I'd like to extend a thank you to the following people for helping me complete this book to tell my story and to help others out there who are just like me.

To my mother, **Trena Kennedy**, and to my stepmother, **Pamela Goldson**, I thank you for giving me the gift of life, always inspiring me to chase my dreams and passing on this gift of poetry. I wouldn't be the man I am today without your love and guidance. Thank you for doing your best to show me the proper way to be the best man I can possibly be and not follow the wrong path in life.

My brother **Cyrus Lowery**, my sister **Zah'bria Epps**, and my godmother **Sheila Epps** have watched me grow over the past eleven years from a wild teenager to a respectable young man. We talk about everything—life, love, family, and more. Your words of advice will always reside with me.

To my sister, **Kennedy McCord**, sometimes I feel that I

failed you growing up because we spent so much time being apart. But I've always loved you just as if you were biologically my little sister. You understand me on a different level and are the only person I can connect with on that level. It's because of you and how you look up to me that I've always felt like a rock star.

Joey Browning, you have been my brother and best friend for almost ten years. You understand me in ways that I never thought of and have always been in my corner, even when some people questioned why you chose to remain friends with someone who has such a different background from you.

Troy Floyd is another close friend I consider my brother, as well as someone I have a great deal of admiration and respect for. Anytime I ever need advice, I can always count on you to give me the honest truth, and just as you of me, I always speak highly of you whenever your name comes up. And to **Mercedez Floyd**, his wife and like a sister to me, I thank you.

I always knew that I had a long lost twin somewhere, and then I met **Darece Garlington**. We're brothers, one and the same—slight differences, but still quite similar. You have always had my back and never made me question your loyalty.

My sister **Jenean Hills** and I talk all the time about everything—religion, life, love, anything that comes up for conversation. I can always count on you for the blunt truth, as well as laughter when I get in that mood to start talking in slogans, which only you can laugh at endlessly.

My brother **Shannon Tyler** is someone I talk to more than expected, since we understand each other in so many various ways. I've given you advice on things, and vice versa.

To **Autumn Bryant**, my close friend, despite our past you continue to provide a level of comfort for me that lets me vent to you, even when I break down or get a little too emotional.

My mentor, **Father Scarborough,** is no longer here with me in physical form, but your guidance has remained with me, and if you were still here, I know you'd be more than proud of the young man I'm becoming as well as what I'm accomplishing. I shared with you my vision of wanting to write a book, but unfortunately you were sent home before I got to this point. Thank you for taking me under your wing when you didn't have to. It meant the world to me, and this book is dedicated to you and our friendship. More than just a friend, you were the father figure I didn't know I needed.

My brother **Roberto DeJesus** is always pushing me to be great and chase what I thought was impossible. We both share a passion for art, and that's why we clicked so well. We also refuse to let each other doubt himself when he's great at what he was born to do.

When it comes to my talent, **Baylee Nicole** is probably one of my biggest fans, as well as someone that looks up to me when it comes to writing poetry. I wouldn't have the faith I have if it wasn't for you and others. I still question the quality of greatness that you see in my talent, but I know it must be great if I inspire you to write as well.

There are more people I'd like to thank, but I can't add everyone's name in the book! But I hope you know you've had a huge impact on my life, and I am far more than just grateful for you all, whether you're family or close friends that I consider my family. You've all helped me to get to this point, and I sincerely hope that I've made you all proud of me. From the bottom of my heart, thank you for everything.

With love,
King Dre Pencasso

Printed in the United States
by Baker & Taylor Publisher Services